STARVE THE POETS!

Yi Sha was born in 1966 in Chengdu, and moved with his family at the age of two to the central Chinese city of Xi'an in Shaanxi province. He published his first poems while still at school, studied Chinese at Beijing Normal University, and became a noted figure among China's university student poets. He has worked on literary magazines, as a TV presenter and independent publisher, and is now an assistant professor at the Xi'an International Studies University.

In 1988 he published a mimeographed first collection, *Lonely Street*, but found an official publisher for his next collection, *Starve the Poets!* (1994). His other poetry and prose titles have included *Vagabond Wharves* (1996), *This Devil Yi Sha* (1998), *The Bastard's Songs* (1999), *Blaspheming Idols* (1999), *Fashion Assassin* (2000), *Critique of 10 Poets* (2001), *My Hero* (2003), *Whoever Hurts, Nows* (2005) and *Shameless Are the Ignorant* (2005). His poetry has been translated into several languages, but he has been refused permission to give readings outside China on a number of occasions. His *Selected Short Poems* was published in a bilingual Chinese-English edition in Hong Kong in 2003. *Starve the Poets!* (Bloodaxe Books, 2008) is his first English publication outside China.

YI SHA
STARVE THE POETS!
SELECTED POEMS

TRANSLATED BY
SIMON PATTON & TAO NAIKAN

BLOODAXE BOOKS

Poems copyright © Wu Wenjian (Yi Sha) 2008
Translations & introduction copyright
© Simon Patton & Tao Naikan 2008

ISBN: 978 1 85224 815 4

First published 2008 by
Bloodaxe Books Ltd,
Highgreen,
Tarset,
Northumberland NE48 1RP.

www.bloodaxebooks.com
For further information about Bloodaxe titles
please visit our website or write to
the above address for a catalogue.

Bloodaxe Books Ltd acknowledges
the financial assistance of
Arts Council England, North East.
Thanks are also due to Arts Council England
for a translation grant for this book.

Cover design: Neil Astley & Pamela Robertson-Pearce.

Printed in Great Britain by
Bell & Bain Limited, Glasgow, Scotland.

CONTENTS

TAO NAIKAN & SIMON PATTON

Introduction: 'There Is Style in the Blood'

Instead of classifying Yi Sha in one line of poetry that stresses 'colloquialism and personal experience of daily life' or in another that advocates 'intellectual writing' and 'the combination of elements of other cultures',[1] we have looked at this poet principally on the basis of our reading of his work itself. Yi Sha once wrote, 'I am writing my own epic in the present tense – an unofficial history in poetry', a statement which indicates his deep concern with the social histories and events of contemporary China. The prominent socio-political significance and historicity of his poetry are qualities reminiscent of Du Fu (712-770), a poet whose work is known as a 'poetic history' of his times. Likewise, the commitment of oneself to recording human mishaps and social turmoil has formed a major part of Yi Sha's poetry, and has enabled him to present a manifold view of social realities and ordinary people in his work. This is largely determined by his attitude toward poetry, for he fervently repudiates not only the fascination in metaphorical and linguistic techniques amongst modern Chinese poets but also the indulgence in sentimental and romantic lyric amongst classical Chinese poets.[2] To him, these types of poets are 'the city's greatest spongers', and, as he accuses in the poem 'Starve the Poets', should deserve starvation to death, including the early Yi Sha.

Two historical events in recent Chinese history reverberate in Yi Sha's poetry. The first is the 'Great Proletarian Cultural Revolution' (1966-76). During the ten years of this mass movement, society was obsessed with the pursuit of the "correct" political line in all aspects of life and driven to a frenzy in the rooting out of class enemies. Photo-records of the period, such as those published in Li Zhensheng's *Red-colour News Soldier*, are typical of the horrific absurdity that gripped China: three Party secretaries stand with enormous, tasselled dunce caps on their heads; seven men stand on chairs in front of a huge crowd, their "crimes" written on placards hung round their necks; a model soldier clutches his copy of the Little Red Book, his uniform and cap decorated with Mao badges of all shapes and sizes... Born in the same year when the Cultural Revolution started, the young Yi Sha must have witnessed more or less of the absurdity and turmoil of this catastrophic era, and it certainly left its mark on his family, as poems such as 'China Punk' and 'The Grudge' show.

Another event fundamentally inspiring to his writing is the June Fourth protest movement of 1989. As Zhang Liang writes in his introduction to *The Tiananmen Papers*, 'June Fourth was not merely a student protest or a patriotic democracy movement. It was the culmination of the biggest, broadest, longest-lasting, and most influential pro-democracy demonstrations anywhere in the world in the 20th century. It also came to a tragic and painful end, in blood and in victory for dictatorship'.[3] Yi Sha's essential poetic orientation – as a poet of ordinary life – is also linked to the momentous events of that Beijing Spring, as is seen in his early poems such as 'Prague Spring' and 'Mild Seven Stars'.

However in most cases, Yi Sha's political sense, regardless of whether it is directed at China or elsewhere, reveals itself in the form of biting satire:

> Back in the old days, we once welcomed
> Nicolae Ceauşescu
> our faces wearing the reserved smiles
> only Chinese children know how to make
> and bobbing in the throng   waving bouquets of flowers
> He smiled   waved at us
> and bent down to kiss
> the luckiest child of them all
> Later, nobody smiled
> A dictator, he was murdered
> by his people
> In the same way we welcomed Ferdinand Marcos
> and Bokassa I of Central Africa
> All these glories once known
> to a Chinese child –
> how they make you cringe with embarrassment
>
> ('Dictators')

These kinds of poems have built up a substantial dimension of his work and formed a rich vein of political satire in it. In addition to socio-political respects, Yi Sha's poetry is also related to the cultural shifts of his time, particularly the so-called 'anti-cultural' (or anti-conventional) tendency of the 1980s, a trend that reacted against the domination of orthodox or mainstream culture as has been exemplified by the music of Cui Jian and the fiction of Wang Shuo.[4] The release in 1986 of Cui Jian's album *Rock and Roll on the New Long March* marked the invention of an authentic Chinese rock'n'roll. The son of a professional trumpet player, Cui developed a distinctive, unlovely vocal style that suggested a refusal to conform to polite norms and artificial good manners. The mangling of language in Cui Jian's delivery, and his emulation of the inarticulate somehow endows his music with a hopeless, awful power that made songs such as 'Nothing to My Name' into anthems of the student protests. The speaker in Yi Sha's poem 'St-stammering, St-stuttering' – 'Saliva f-f-flying in all directions / You all smell so old and stale' – is Cui Jian translated into poetry. Marginality, alienation, anger at the existing order, a heroic, pointless refusal of all social pieties, all these features are common ground shared by the two artists. Rock amounts to rebellion, and embraces the personal as much as the political.

The stance Yi Sha has assumed as a poet is that of ordinary people (see his poem 'The Common People') rather than that of the elevated intellectual. This standpoint basically determines the perspective from which he speaks. In this regard, he is one of the successors to a line of poetry initiated by Han Dong and Yu Jian. Nevertheless, the poetic persona in his work, who is in his case always a first person 'I', is a holistic human in the sense that it speaks not only of the good in humanity and society but also of evils, both of the 'upper part of the body' (which, in current Chinese parlance, refers to abstract thought) and of the 'lower part of the body' (human nature and desires). As the persona in the poem 'Principle' declares: 'With me I carry spirit, faith, soul, / thought, desire, perversion, malice, B.O. / They dwell as parasites in this house of me: / I treat them all even-handedly'.

11

Because of this outlook, there is a confessional ele-ment in Yi Sha: many negative aspects of his experience have a chance of finding their way into his writing. In the poem 'At the Zoo', for example, it is the cruelty of his young son that the persona feels driven to describe. In 'Collusion', he ruthlessly dissects his own motives for giving money to a beggar. Moreover, in 'Old Tolstoy Ticked Me Off', he catches himself enjoying a telecast of the Iraq War and, with punishing honesty, tries to record the rebuke his own conscience delivers to him.

A curious feature of Yi Sha's early poetry is his insistence on illegitimacy. Although, by his own admission, he was born into a relatively happy intellectual family ('I grew up in a typical intellectual family, a family with typically loving parents. My father and mother were devoted to one another and there was never any talk of divorce...'), *Starve the Poets* includes numerous references to the poet's bastard status. In China, the ritual pre-sentation of namecards is an indispensable act of social interaction: it is simple, indisputable evidence of a person's professional position. Yi Sha's poetic namecard – a spare two lines which read 'You may be So-and-So's son-in-law / but I am Father to my self' ('Namecard') – recasts his "stigma" in a wholly positive light. It is as an act of independent creation. Another poem entitled 'The Bastard's Song' (not included in this selection) sums up the predicament in a stark play on words: the poet 'was both flame and blame' [*huo he huo*] to one young unmarried couple. In the final lines of the same poem he explicitly links his legitimacy as a writer to his bastardy: 'the Great Poet Yi Sha wrote: "I am Father to my self".' At the time he was writing, Yi Sha wished to disassociate himself from the Chinese mainstream of writers, and his claim to illegitimacy is perhaps best understood as an expression of estrangement – as well as of rebelliousness.

Furthermore, in his work Yi Sha also extends his sense of personal illegitimacy to include prostitutes, beggars, drinkers, punks, rapists, convicted criminals, stutterers, the addicted, the mute, and the blind. By presenting them as so many 'wounds' of humanity and society – a view that is implied in the poem 'The Wound's Song' and that is clearly illustrated in many of his poems focusing on hospitals and patients – Yi Sha gives them an essential role to play in his 'unofficial history'. While seeing such 'wounds' as part of society, or as evils inherent in human nature, Yi Sha also lays stress on sexuality in his writing, seeing it as part and parcel of human nature. To him, sexuality may perform various roles in his writing. For example, it is used ironically in 'International Year of Peace', and elsewhere, it evokes the alienation of human beings or the fraught relationship between the sexes (see 'The Force of a Detail').

This aspect of his poetry, an intensive emphasis on one's private life, may be considered to be a poetic practice, precedent and inspiring to the notion of the 'lower part of the body' (*xia ban shen*), and this helps to illustrate the change that has taken place in current Chinese poetry and literature. The notion of *xia ban shen* is derived from the concept of '*shenti xiezuo*' (writing from the body), a term used in both commercial promotion and literary criticism of such quasi-biographical novels as *Shanghai baobei* (Shanghai baby) by Wei Hui and *Tang* (Lollies) by Mianmian.[5] Although these 'privacy-exposing' novels are considered to be 'sexual' and highly commercial, they were very popular and influential at the turn of the 20th and 21st centuries, and exerted an influence on poetry. Evidence of this was the transformation of the successful column entitled *Pengyoumen* (friends) in the poetry website *Shi jianghu* (the folk world of poetry), and the change of its name to *Xia ban shen* (the lower half of the body) in 2000.[6] This not only signalled the influence of fiction on poetry, but also the extreme to which a number of poets would go from 'writing from the body' to writing from its lower part. Some poets asserted that the 'upper part of the body', the mind, had been 'polluted and alienated' by the education they have received and by the cultural traditions they have inherited, and that since the mind to them prevented the creation of anything new, it had to be abandoned in favour of the vitality and desires of the lower part.[7]

With regard to Yi Sha's concise and direct style, conception plays a crucial role: it is the idea of the poem that primarily drives it, rather than a distinctive linguistic manner. Style, he once wrote, is not something he deliberately strives for: it is in the blood. At its best, the simplicity of style and the charm of the conceit complement one another perfectly. Something close to perfection is achieved in an early poem entitled 'Factory for Artificial Limbs':

> I was friends with Chen Xiangdong when we were kids
> These days he works in a factory
> that makes artificial limbs
> One day, he called me out of the blue
> and we arranged to meet
> I recognised him   waiting at the factory gates
> his smiling face was exactly the same as before
> only magnified a couple of times
> I noticed something odd about the way he walked
> so I pulled up one leg of his trousers
> It's real, he laughed
> We only remembered to shake hands
> as the two of us began to move off
> He squeezed my hand with his fingers
> Still intact, just like the good old days
> Everything was intact, same as it ever was
> We both roared with laughter

This is a deft poem about friendship. Despite the gap in their relationship and the threat of artificiality, the men quickly recover the bond that brought them together in the first place all those years ago: the bond of humour. The banter they enjoy in one another's company, and the uproarious natural laughter it provokes, is proof that their friendship has survived.

This directness simplifies the translator's task in some ways. Nevertheless, Yi Sha's concision and plain-spoken expression are frequently interwoven with idioms, colloquialisms, slang and vulgar expressions, used to heighten and intensify the vivacity of his ideas and the authenticity of daily lives. Rendering such idiosyncratic features of the Chinese – while maintaining sufficient interest to excite an English-language reader – is a very daunting challenge.

Yi Sha's performance of illegitimacy has, as he predicted, brought him a certain degree of acceptance as a poet. Since the publication of his first collection, *Starve the Poets*, in 1994, he has published a steady stream of new work, and has established himself as a controversial and unavoidable presence in the domain of Chinese poetry. His success is, perhaps, proof of his own maxim: 'The time to "starve the poets" is on its way. True poets "starve" but they "do not die"!'

This selection is largely based on a selection of over 340 poems sent to us by the poet, who had written them between 1988 and 2007. The selection is arranged chronologically to give an idea of his development, and includes, we hope, a fairly representative sample of Yi Sha's various moods and modes. In a note written to accompany his first published book of poems Yi Sha quipped: 'We cannot live like human beings, but we can write like them.' As translators, we have done our best to hold onto the human despite all the challenges posed by the cultural divide, and we wish that this translation might bring readers closer to knowledge of contemporary China.[8]

NOTES

1. Chen Chao: 'Chongzhu shige de lishi xiangxiangli' (Reconstruction of the historical imagination in poetry) in Lin Jianfa, (ed.) *21 shiji Zhongguo wenxue daxi: 2006 nian wenxue piping* (21st-century Chinese literature series: 2006 literary criticism), (Shenyang: Chunfeng wenyi Press, 2007): p. 225.

2. Yi Sha, 'Preface' to *Starve the Poets* (Beijing: Zhongguo huaqiao chubanshe, 1994), pp. 170-73.

3. Zhang Liang: *The Tiananmen Papers* (London: Little, Brown, 2001).

4. Wang Shuo's influence is seen in the cool hippie-like manner of his speaking and in his phraseology, as shown in the poem title 'Wo shi liangmin wo pa shui' (I'm a law-abiding citizen, I'm not afraid of anybody) which was derived from Wang's phrase 'Wo shi liumang wo pa shui' (I'm a hooligan, I'm not afraid of anybody).

5. The phrase 'writing from the body' may have been derived from Mianmian's remarks: 'using the body to examine men, and using the skin to think'. See Shao Yanjun, 'Meinu wenxue' xianxiang yanjiu (A case-study of 'beauty-literature' phenomenon), Guilin: Guangxi Normal University Press, 2005: p. 32, pp. 58-59.

6. See Yi Sha, 'Xianchang muji: 2000 nian Zhongguo xinshi guanjianci' (Witness on the spot: key words for 2000 new Chinese poetry), in Yang Ke, (ed.) *2000 Zhongguo xinshi nianjian* (2000 almanac of new Chinese poetry), (Guangzhou Press, 2000): p. 428.

7. See Shen Haobo, 'Xiabanshen xiezuo ji fandui shangbanshen' (Writing from the lower part of the body and objection to the upper part of the body), Duo Yu, 'Wo xianzai kaolu de 'xia ban shen'' ('The lower part of the body' I am thinking about), in Yang Ke, (ed.) *2000 Zhongguo xinshi nianjian* (2000 almanac of new Chinese poetry), (Guang-zhou Press, 2000): p. 546, pp. 560-64.

8. The translators would like to thank Gavin O'Toole of Aflame Books for allowing us to include a revised version of 'Urban Landscape', first published in *Che in Verse* in 2007. We would also like to thank the organisers of the Rotterdam Poetry International Festival for letting us include four poems – 'Police Car, Poet, Snow', 'I'm a Law-abiding Citizen: I'm Not Afraid of Anyone', 'Spring's Breast-cancer Disaster' and 'Bombs and Poetry' – earlier versions of which were translated for Yi Sha's visit to Rotterdam in 2007 for the 38th Poetry International Festival.

The translators and Yi Sha would like to acknowledge here the very special role Naomi Jaffa of The Poetry Trust has played in this project. Her initial idea to invite Yi Sha to Aldeburgh Poetry Festival (and the idea dates back to 2005) and her enthusiasm for a collection of translations has been the guiding inspiration for this book.

STARVE THE POETS!

Crossing the Yellow River

As the train was passing over the Yellow River
I was in the toilet having a piss
Oh, I knew I was being remiss
I should have been sitting at one of the windows
or standing by a door of the carriage
left hand on my hip
shielding my eyes with my right hand
gazing out   like some Great Man
or like a poet, at the very least
recalling some anecdote connected with this river
or some episode from its history
Just then, everyone was gazing out the window
while I was in the toilet
for what seemed like ages
for my time had come
I had waited 24 hours for this
but in the time it took to have a piss
I'd left the Yellow River a long way behind me

[1988]

No. 9

On the gate of No. 9 a black padlock rusts
In a window at No. 9 a bra hangs all year round, swaying to
      and fro
In the yard of No. 9 you can smell the scent of sophora buds
      in spring
At No. 9 you can hear snatches of song at night
The dog at No. 9 comes and goes through a flap in the gate
In the letterbox at No. 9 the mail sleeps soundly
The lawn of No. 9 stretches all the way down to the asphalt-
      covered street
The sun at No. 9 goes to bed early and gets up late
In this world of wind and dust the beauties of No. 9 have faded
As the twilight falls tonight
there's a knock on the door at No. 9 –
a pair of gumboots stands on the doorstep

[1989]

Wishful Thinking or the Feelings You Get from a Film Played Backwards

A shell is fired back into the barrel of a gun
Writing is sucked back into the tip of a pen
Snow floats from the ground
Daytime rushes towards the sun
Rivers run to their sources
Trains creep inside tunnels
Ruins pick themselves off the ground and stand tall as buildings
Machines break down into their component bits
A child crawls into its mother's womb
Pedestrians vanish off the streets
Dead leaves spring onto branches
The girl who committed suicide does a backward leap onto the
        second floor
The lost man jumps down from the poster seeking his
        whereabouts
The hand that stretches out to others is tucked back into its
        pocket
The bride runs away from the marriage bed
and turns into a young girl in love for the very first time
Youth grows innocent
till it sucks on rubber nipples thicker than cigarettes
She too comes back
walking in reverse
to my cramped room
I will walk away from that chilly
unfamiliar railway station
and go back to the classroom
my red Pioneer's scarf knotted round my neck
standing to greet my teachers   working at my lessons
getting ahead   studying hard

[1989]

21

Night Blackout

Blackout tonight:
city blanketed in darkness
but even so
my eyes continue to work
after a fashion
I can visualise
the candles in the drawer
the drawer in the cupboard
the cupboard in a corner of the room
In the dark
I walked over to the cupboard
pulled open the drawer
and took out a candle
I did all these things without much trouble
On my way back, however
I stumbled and fell
not because I tripped
but because
I closed my eyes

[1989]

A Shocking Sight

I saw
a beggar with filthy hands
fingering a coin
fingering
the chilly national emblem
on it

[1989]

Miracle

The ears of wheat
on the coins in my pocket
have ripened

As I walked down the street
I mumbled a phrase to myself
I'm not sure
what it meant

All anyone could smell
was the sweet scent of wheat
No one had the faintest idea
that this miracle
was my doing

Lighting a Cigarette for a Truck Driver

It's a kind of ritual
lighting a cigarette for a truck driver
is a kind of rite
I held it between my lips as I lit up
inhaled deeply
then placed it in his mouth
I did this
as the truck turned a corner
and another stretch of road went by
Had he braked suddenly
I could have lost my balance
and whacked my head
against the windscreen
but he didn't
He kept his eyes on the road
aware of what I was doing
He moved his lips as a sign to me
If I'd been a woman
the gesture wouldn't have meant anything
My being a man
only made the rite more profound
The road is long and uncertain   Mr Driver
this small life of mine
is entirely in your hands

[1990]

A Smoker Thinks Back

It was a summer night in '72
A giant of a man walked past
in the street
Me   a six-year-old kid
went and picked up the butt he had tossed on the ground
It was still burning
As I sucked on it   my eyes narrowed like slits
and since then, no matter what the brand
I wear the same expression whenever I smoke a cigarette
It was like the first time I had sex
I'll always remember the name
of that very first flame of mine

[1990]

Whistling

My big sis is sleeping in the wheat fields
with a man

With a slingshot in my hand
I'm up a tree, whistling

There's no sign of Ma
I'm still whistling

Whistling...

For years
whenever my sister heard me whistle

she'd break down and cry

[1990]

My Life as a Monk

I spend my days
   as a monk
   ringing chimes

Passing the time
   with other monks
   fetching water

For you my love
   I had my head shaved
   and took my vows
to redeem my soul

Look at these beads
   in my hand
on this sunlit
   morning

How they shine
How they shine

[1990]

Prague Spring

Prague's Spring
is not over there   Flowers bloom
on the borders of this nation
I was the young man who stood in the path
of the tanks in the centre of the Square
on his own
The Czech Republic – homeland of the Spring
The swallows of freedom
have all flown away again
never once looking back
The girl with the blue eyes I am deeply
in love with   sobs
in the April breeze
I am the young man who stood in the path
of the tanks on his own
questioned by a Russian soldier
who shouted at him sternly
How come   you Chinese
love poking your noses into other people's business so much?

[1991]

31

Dictators

Back in the old days, we once welcomed
Nicolae Ceauşescu
our faces wearing the reserved smiles
only Chinese children know how to make
and bobbing in the throng   waving bouquets of flowers
He smiled   waved at us
and bent down to kiss
the luckiest child of them all
Later, nobody smiled
A dictator, he was murdered
by his people
In the same way we welcomed Ferdinand Marcos
and Bokassa I of Central Africa
All these glories once known
to a Chinese child –
how they make you cringe with embarrassment

[1991]

St-stammering, St-stuttering

I st-stammer, st-stutter
S-s-second-class disability
Can't control my r-r-rushing thoughts
Nor my legs

Saliva f-f-flying in all directions
You all smell so old and stale
M-m-my poor lungs
How hard they have to slave!

I have to g-g-get away from this
Your st-st-strange
Rhythms
I can hardly wait to break free

M-m-my
Machine-gun-like language
F-f-fires in bursts
Full of pleasure

St-stammering, st-stuttering, my fate
But there are n-n-no ghosts in my way
L-l-look at me, I say
There's only indifference on my face

[1991]

The High Tower

In the instant I moved into that high tower
doomed to collapse in ten seconds
but still nine seconds away
from my fatal heart attack
I'd have to say I was a happy man...

10 – 9 – 8 – 7 – 6
5 – 4 – 3 – 2 – 1

While in the instant I moved into that high tower
doomed to collapse in nine seconds
but still ten seconds away
from my fatal heart attack
I couldn't honestly call myself unhappy

[1991]

Comfort for the Future

On the day the Bastille was stormed
a child's shoe was found abandoned
in a boulevard

The following morning
my son came home, sneaking
into his room

his one foot bare

[1991]

Golden Autumn

I cannot stop the autumn leaves
falling to the ground
I cannot stop
the opened newspaper
fluttering like a funeral banner
in the autumn wind
An old man sits
on a park bench
his walking stick fallen on the ground beside him
I cannot stop
the misery he feels
as he thinks back to the days of the Soviet Union

[1991]

I Am a Wrongly-written Chinese Character

I am a wrongly-written Chinese character
on a blackboard in some village primary school
I can't remember   whose hand it was that wrote me
or exactly what year it was
I anxiously look out at those children
They stare up at me with perfect trust
A wrongly-written Chinese character
leading generations of young kids astray
One year   I don't remember when
a teacher from some place else came along
and rubbed me out with her delicate hand
and I turned into a swirl of chalk dust
inside her sun-filled lungs

[1991]

Namecard

You may be So-and-So's son-in-law
but I am Father to my self

[1991]

The Nobel Prize in Literature:
A Thank-you Speech for Eternity

I won't turn it down   I'm eager, of course
to accept this money made from the sale of dynamite
I'll spend the whole lot on explosives
Your Highness, Carl XVI Gustaf, King of Sweden
my esteemed Ladies and Gentlemen
could I please ask you to make yourselves ready?
Would you all please

HIT THE GROUND!

[1992]

Traitor

He shows his face in a foreign country
sitting in the second row
of a temporary grandstand
at a football match
He's a middle-aged man
wearing dark glasses
with his hair evenly parted
He is watching the team
of the country he has betrayed
compete
His small-footed kinsmen
aren't faring too well
but the traitor
waves his flag, cheers
and keeps in high spirits
He lives overseas now
and is leader
of the cheer squad
When China
the country that has issued a warrant for his arrest
sees his face
on TV
it's beyond a joke, really:
you don't know whether to laugh or cry

[1992]

Learning a Trade from a Master Carpenter

This morning, as a cool breeze blows against his cheeks
the apprentice carpenter learns a new skill

The Master gives him a private lesson
showing him how to make coffins

What for? What for?
Eyes wide open   He works hard to learn and keeps asking
          questions

For no reason at all! the Master answers
Coffins are dead easy

[1992]

My Ideal Readers

I think I could find
ideal readers for my poetry
among English football hooligans
among the fans of the Hillbilly Cat
among black South Africans
Polish workers
South Korean students
and the illustrious citizens of Beijing
All these are my ideal readers
– I guess
I should get going right away
in search of them
taking a book of my poems with me
reading it to them
and getting involved in whatever they're doing
– I guess
the first person my work might touch
could be a drunken bum
from Russia

[1993]

Up, Up and Away

An addict
is dead
four days after
going off drugs
He died in rehab
His family
feels inexpressible relief
free at last
I
was a friend of his
Out on the streets
I suddenly look up
and see him
hurtling across the sky
just like Superman –
up, up, and away

[1993]

Would President Clinton Please Fill in the Blanks

A plane with US markings zooms across the sky
It drops [   ] on the Balkans
where civil war is breaking out everywhere
and the flames of conflict rage
Would the President please select one of the following
alternatives
to show how he would solve
the problem of the former Yugoslavia:

(1) bombs   (2) food   (3) J.B. Tito

[1994]

China Punk

It was pure rock'n'roll

30 years ago
a few Red Guards
forcibly cut my grandfather's hair

in a bizarre style
neither male nor female, neither human nor freak
It was pretty similar to a style now popular

with Chinese punk rockers: only his was 30 years ago

(1994]

Confessions

I would never be so pedantic
as to confess to killing a fly
but I did
squash a pair
in the act of making love

[1994]

Destiny

Ages ago, I got the hang of what it means to be human:
on a merry-go-round in a public park
an abandoned child wrapped in baby clothes
wears a blank expression on its face
as the sun rises brilliantly in the east

[1994]

Sunday

In a book on art
I came across
two paintings by Van Gogh
which hadn't been mounted on banknotes
These two celebrated works
were unremarkable paintings
One was called 'Gauguin's Chair'
The other
was called 'Van Gogh's Chair'
Although I didn't go so far
as to buy the book
I was
so moved by what I saw
that –
like 'a chariot driven south
to get north' –
I got on the wrong trolley-bus
for home

[1994]

The International Year of Peace

Impatient after a short separation
we start making love in the lounge
The TV is on
showing scenes of destruction
What caused the war?
We look like two kids
who find themselves in serious trouble
We look at each other:
what the hell are we going to do?

[1995]

The X-Ray

He was shaking
throughout the X-ray
The doctor noticed
his trembling
He could also see
that a man's shaking
starts in his bones

[1995]

50

In Reply to My Mother

I was sitting with my mother
watching TV   This has become
a rare thing for us

On telly, the hero
got trapped in a fire
and was horribly disfigured

My mother warned me:
'If you ever find yourself in a similar situation
you must never get involved…'

I sat there staring at her
I was speechless   This has become
a rare thing for us

She had forgotten
how she had taught me to behave
how she had taught me to behave as an adult

'Don't worry, Mum
I wouldn't help anyone in a fire
even if it was me who was burning'

This seemed to satisfy her
When the program was over
she went and stewed some spareribs for me

[1995]

Why I Lost the Power of Speech

Because we had moved into a new flat
and had bought new furniture
we called in a painter
a deaf-mute

The kind look on his face
was reassuring

As he worked
I'd talk quite openly
with my wife
about his ability as a painter
and how
we were would try
to knock down his price a bit

He couldn't hear us
That's the thing with deaf-mutes
They can't hear

My wife learnt quite a bit of sign language
from our painter
which showed her knack for getting on with people
In the large wardrobe mirror
I'd watch her talking with the deaf-mute
observing her animated body language
and the look on her face growing kinder by the minute

Long after he'd finished
and had left
without a word
with his money

my wife continued to communicate with me
using sign language

I had no wish to talk, either
I had lost the power of speech

[1995]

Waiting for Godot

In a small theatre
used by an experimental theatre group

Waiting for Godot
is being performed

So old-hat
The audience is miniscule

They wait and they wait
Godot doesn't show up

Realising he won't come
no one's really waiting

Some people start to nod off
It's precisely at this moment, however

right at the end of the play
that someone runs onto the stage

This unexpected 'unexpected twist'
really gets the crowd going

The interloper
turns out to be the idiot son of the doorkeeper

There's no way to stop him
He dashes to the middle of the stage

He yells 'Uncle!' at the crowd
and bawls his eyes out, demanding sweets

'Godot's turned up!'
Thunderous applause: the audience jumps to its feet

[1995]

The Wound's Song

My horror of wounds:
  to find them
    spitting blood
    like mouths

My greater horror of wounds:
  those that reveal bone
    baring
    teeth

The wounds that cover my body:
  they laugh
    and sing

[1995]

My Son's Loneliness

He's six months old
when my son sees himself in the big wardrobe mirror for the
        first time
He thinks it's someone else

Another toddler the same height
stands before him
I'm delighted by the scene   It's as if
I had two sons – twin brothers

Together the two dance
babbling in unison   Then they
hold out small hands to each other
and touch palms   *That's settled, then*

My son's loneliness
is the loneliness all only children feel
together with most of humanity

[1996]

57

At the Zoo

I haven't been to this zoo for 18 years
On this visit here today
I've brought my young son along to see
that there are other creatures on this planet besides us humans
In the tiger enclosure   The animal here now
is not the one I knew 18 years ago
That was this one's mother
It died one summer ten years ago
That's not important
All my son needs to know
is that it's a tiger
Later, when it growls
my son starts bawling
so I take him away
to look at the spotted deer
Because I coax it
with a handful of grass
it pushes its muzzle
up against the railing
As it does this
my fearless son grabs at its head
with his tiny fingers
and pokes it viciously in the eyes

[1996]

Holiday

The fireworks of these prosperous times
calmly extinguish in a monk's eyes

The fireworks of these prosperous times:
he turns his back on tonight's sky

[1996]

The Grateful Drunk

A drunk
was vomiting   in the city
vomiting in the rich glow of the setting sun
on a bridge on the city moat
There was no end to it   He looked like
he was singing at the top of his lungs
He threw up what he'd eaten
bile, even
On my way home from work
I stopped   and took in this sight
I suddenly felt deeply moved
It occurred to me that everyone has their own unique way
of showing gratitude to life

[1996]

Suicide Kid

Water-pistol in hand
the kid
ambushed us
out of the blue
Clearly
he liked that gun of his
shooting at us
until we pretended to panic
and ran off screaming
The kid laughed his head off
He looked like such a hero

Later
we saw him again
at dusk
alone in the glow of the setting sun
sitting on the grass
pointing the pistol at himself
He put it in his mouth
with rapt concentration
no longer interested in us

There's something strange about that kid
you said   I knew
what you meant
but since he lived next-door to me
I knew what was really going on:
every time his mother came out
she would fill his water-pistol
with milk

However
I kept
this detail from you
to save you from disappointment

[1997]

61

Hong Kong 1997

When you were poor
you sold off your own child

As his mother
you couldn't bring yourself to say
he'd been captured by bandits

But now he's back
The child you sold off
with a straw 'for sale' sign on his head
is back

A smart gentleman
wearing a Western-style suit and leather shoes
now sits opposite you
his glossy hair slicked back, his chin shaved

I seem to hear him say:
'I am now just a guest
in my parents' home'

[1997]

Sunflower in the Bathroom

I was lying in the bath-tub
soaking in hot water
shaped something like a hippo
but feeling like a god

The sound of something moving
caught my attention
got me alert: above me
the sunflower shower nozzle
was turning, creaking
towards the one source of light
in the bathroom:
the sunlamp

As soon as I saw it
I went ice-cold all over:
an astonished hippo
leapt out of the water –
a man sprinting naked
from the bathroom
No one could understood
what it actually was
that had given him such a scare

[1997]

The Force of a Detail

She remembered that kiss

not because
the movement between his tongue and lips
gave her any special feeling
but because
as the other interested party
he had wiped
the back of his hand across his mouth
when he was done

as if he'd just finished eating

[1998]

The Only Face I Remembered That Year

To describe him as 'repulsively ugly and sly'
would be appropriate
as well as convenient and simple
but how irresponsible
It would amount to saying nothing
because you still wouldn't know
what he actually looked like
Over the past year
his is the only face I remember
out of all the strangers I've seen
emaciated   the face of an ordinary worker
by a crematorium furnace
That day   I was pushing
the corpse of my mother along on a trolley
when he blocked my path and said
'Leave it to me. There's nothing more for you to do here.'
I gave him the box
of 555 cigarettes I had brought with me
This he took without the slightest reaction
and turned away, pushing the trolley
the man who was to give my mother her send off

[1998]

Common Sense

On the street
in a sweltering summer heatwave

a young girl hops
a hand over one ear

Her behaviour is a little odd
In her case, there's a certain beauty to it

Oddness and a so-called beauty –
this gives people

the feelings they want
but they pay no attention

to the cause and the source
of her actions

But I know
because to me it's only common sense

As a boy
on my way home from the swimming pool

I used the same movement
to help me get rid of

any last remaining water in my ear
It would trickle away hotly

and I would be able to hear the world again
just like this young girl here

I'm sure she's feeling pretty good
right now

hopping with a hand over one ear
on the street in a sweltering summer heatwave

Common sense like this
has helped me find my way to an essential poetry

[1998]

Salute

The streets are perfectly straight
The boulevards stretch all the way to the horizon
Pedestrians move towards me
in a compact mass
Who is it that compels me
to raise my hand to my forehead
and fills me with a sense of respect?
                    A pregnant woman
like a penguin treading on ice:
so beautiful
so happy and proud

[1998]

Childhood Thirst

At the outside tap
I bend down
stretch out my neck
and twist my head
Childhood thirst
The water trickles down
with a splash
In that moment
I drink some water
refreshing my mouth
In that moment
I see a view
I see people
I see
the world in front of my eyes
not upside-down
of course
not right way up
but slant

[1999]

One-touch Ball Contact

Many years ago
a football coach
(who was in fact
a high school sports teacher)
explained the theory
of one-touch ball contact to me
He said that receiving the ball
and passing it
had to be done in the one motion
A most
rational movement
which reduced to a minimum
the time spent holding onto
the ball
Dribbling was even less desirable
What he said in conclusion
he said standing up
His voice
rang out over that
high school football pitch
He said: Your aim
is to get the ball
into the zone most dangerous to the opposition
in the shortest possible time
with a minimum of movement
Later
although I never managed
to make a living out of soccer
as he had hoped
there's no doubt
that his theory found its way
into my writing

[1999]

Diary

On one day in my life
(Could it have really been thus?)

I wrote poetry in the morning
I wrote poetry in the afternoon
and that evening
I was still writing

On one day in my life
(Goodness! Just one single day)

[1999]

Pain at First-hand

Writhing on the floor in agony
from gallstones
helped me to understand Ernest Hemingway
It convinced me
that this famous clever dick
blew half his head off with his hunting shotgun
not because of impotence
but from pain

[1999]

The Grudge

My grandpa could never forget it
Close to death, he still bore a grudge
The man who, in 1968,
had whipped him to the ground
with a leather belt
and stopped him ever getting to his feet again
was not a soldier or a policeman
He was a man who wore glasses

My grandpa could never forget it
Close to death, he still bore his grudge

[1999]

Outer Suburbs: An Abandoned Railway Carriage

An outer suburb:
an abandoned railway carriage
shunted onto a section
of abandoned track
came into view
in the twilight gloom
I also saw
a man
sneak into it
closely followed
by a woman
An abandoned
railway carriage
shunted onto a section
of abandoned track
also carries the weight of
fervent lives
like someone
unwilling to abandon their last years
or someone
abandoned by fate but not yet done with
The sound of a disused train whistle
rang in my ears

[2000]

In a Time More Enduring than a Moment

Speeding along the highway
past fields, villages
cities, towns and factories
When a church with a steeple
suddenly comes into view
you cry out loud
then fall silent
No one else in the car
could imagine
how this had plunged you
into a state of solemnity
or that what this brought you
was a happiness you needed
to savour quietly
A happiness
in a time more enduring
than a moment

[2000]

The Dialysis Centre

A small, isolated building
shaped like a mouth

I knew there was life inside
Life that could be bought with cash

My mother said no
to the transaction

Suffering from uraemia
she said no to dialysis

and no to having her blood
filtered

Her faith
was straightforward and simple

She said we all have to die sooner or later
She had no wish to leave my father

a poor old man
without a cent to his name

As her son, what hurt me
was that even if I had gone all out to earn money

I could never have filled that mouth
that mouth that spews out life

[2000]

Principle

With me I carry spirit, faith, soul,
thought, desire, perversion, malice, B.O.

They dwell as parasites in this house of me:
It is my duty to treat them all even-handedly

[2000]

My Grandmother's Presence

I was my grandmother's pet
from what my mother tells me
Me, I don't remember
I can't remember a single thing about her
but watching the way my mother
dotes on her grandson
I'm convinced
there was once a woman like her in this world
who loved me so much
with that special love only old women
are capable of
For me
my grandmother's presence
only means that when my mother has forebodings
about one thing or another
she drags me over to my grandmother's photograph
and forces me to talk to her
In a hoarse, quacking voice
I say to her out loud: Nanna,
please look after our family
It works every time
My mother explains it like this: Your Nanna
always did what you told her to
and she'll always looks after the family
from up there in Heaven

[2000]

Collusion

He comes and asks me for money
because, right beside me,
stands
a pretty woman.

I give him money
because that pretty woman
who stands there next to me
is watching

[2000]

Small Town Story

When the man squatting
outside the small hotel
lights up his third cigarette
there's a whiff of anxiety in it
He'd like to go up and see
his wife in the upstairs room
but he senses how inappropriate
that would be
The man squatting
outside the small hotel
works so hard
pimping for his own wife
I think he must be
the coollest
(or is he the cruellest?) man
in the world

Small street   small town
A train
pulls up for a minute
farts a couple of times
Toot toot!
then leaves with a noise
like crying

[2000]

MTV

He dances to a music of illusions
then walks off

to the main road
and on to the petrol station
where he picks up a can of petrol
then keeps on going

He crosses a vast plain
passes a solitary white house
and heads for a forest
Sun shines among the branches

Our singer
keeps going
He may not be a pretty-boy dimwit
but for sure he's a cool arsehole

On he goes
A shot is inserted here
to show that the can of petrol
has been leaking the whole way

There is petrol in the grass like dew
and petrol on the road like drops of water
The scenes flash back
I know what the director has in mind

Sure enough
At the end of the road
when the last drop of petrol has dripped from the can
he flicks on his cigarette lighter

And so it happens
a line of flame burns all the way back
to where he started from

[2000]

Memories of Red China

Looking like hearses,
the refrigerated vans
delivering meat products
crawled along
the near-deserted boulevards
At every intersection
youths with heads too big for their bodies
squatted on street corners
swallowing their saliva in silence

[2000]

My Father's Not a Well Man But He's Still a Man

Dad, even if you weighed more than you do
I'd still find a way to lift you
This is what a son is capable of
when it comes to the crunch
When you got back to the ward
from the operating theatre
it was me who lifted you onto your bed
I did this
while you were naked
There were large yellow bandages
covering your belly
A thick-tubed catheter was attached
to your shrunken penis
The young female nurse
was the only woman present
and so there was nothing to be embarrassed about
After I'd exerted myself to the utmost
in the execution of this action
all that remained to do
was to cover you up with a white cotton sheet
As I did so, you laughed
This was a result of the anaesthetic
You hadn't yet lost that feeling of euphoria
and felt no sense of loss
for the left-kidney they had removed
but feeling aggrieved you grumbled:
'Those women shaved off my pubic hair!'

[2001]

You Have To Be Reminded to Love Life

On the eve of the Spring Festival
I was doing some shopping at the supermarket
my son in a trolley
with the various things I'd bought
He was nibbling on chocolate
and was nearly falling asleep
Lying there
he looked like a little Buddha
People were smiling
at him
There was one old man
who just wouldn't go away
He squatted down
in front of the trolley to look at my son
and asked me:
'How much
does a son cost?'
His tone of voice
and the look on his face
suddenly
brought the spirit of the Spring Festival
home to me
and I made up my mind then and there
to enjoy New Year to the max

[2001]

The Facts of Life

When I was little, I asked my father:
'Dad
where did I come from?'
He told me:
'From a gob of spit'
I committed his reply to memory
this response concerning
the facts of life

Years later, my son asked me the same question:
'Dad
where did I come from?'
I gave him the same answer
'From a gob of spit'
I recalled what my father had said to me
and remembered
that he had always been straight with me

My son, however,
was not as trusting
as I had been at his age
When he heard what I had to say
he jumped to his feet
and shouted:
'But the teacher told us
spitting wasn't allowed!'

[2001]

Crossing the Stage

I don't think
I'll ever forget
the man before me now

Walking across life's stage

Just now
as I handed him a cigarette
he gave me a light

Walking across life's stage

In the flickering flames
I got a glimpse of his cigarette lighter –
well, what d'you know?: it was shaped like a mini-
fire extinguisher

[2001]

This Poem Isn't About a Pretty Female Friend or a Soulmate

My dear
dear
friend
Why do others
only see the brothel in me
while you always manage to find
the temple in my soul
and even hear
the ringing of its bells?

[2001]

Mild Seven Stars

Written for a student leader during the 1989 Tiananmen Incident

I never liked her tarty manner
and she loathed my show of gentlemanly good behaviour
When the storm of the age broke
she revolted
I wavered

But when
this woman caught up in the high-pitch of revolution
tossed me a pack of Mild Seven Stars as she left
without once looking back
I was sure she must've meant something by it

I did not see her good looks on the wanted posters
nor did I hear any mention of her in the rumours going round
I shared that pack of Mild Sevens
with some friends of mine at uni
but I never smoked that brand again

[2001]

Dumplings

Even on the last day of the lunar year
he and his father were hard at work
labouring in the fields from dawn to dusk
That is the reason why
he has such a clear recollection of the very last sunset
of the Year of the Snake
Back home
his mother served up a meal
of steaming hot dumplings
After dinner he went straight to bed
because he and his father
had to go back into the fields again the following day
This he had to do
because the university fees he needed to pay each year
came (and could only come)
from tilling the soil

A university student
from a village
recounted to everyone present
how he spent his New Year's Eve
as an exercise in oral presentation skills
in my class
In the five minutes he took to tell his story
his delivery was smooth, steady
his tone was detached
It was only when he got
to the word 'dumplings'
that a smile crept over his face

[2002]

89

An E-mail I Never Sent G.

Things are not quite the way
you predicted they would be
On the road to fame and fortune
I still think of you
As I was taking a walk
in a residential area
in countryside in the south of Sweden
it occurred to me that you would like
these timber houses
painted so charmingly
Families of three
dwell inside in them
have little to do with the outside world
and are left in peace
Perhaps in my next life, then
sweetheart
In my present life
I am a grotty, unregulated, substandard poet
in love
with this grotty, unregulated, substandard motherland of ours
We are inseparable
In my next life
I'll try to come back as a Swedish doctor
but will still marry you
and give you a life like this

[2002]

Exchange

In Nässjö, in a park by a lake
a black headscarf cannot wrap away her beauty –
the Arab woman on the swing

When I walked up to her
she spoke to me
in English
I misunderstood
thinking she wanted me to keep away
wanted this good-for-nothing
this trouble-maker
to leave her alone

As I hesitated
I made sense of the last part
of what she was saying
She was asking
whether I wanted a turn on the swing
What she meant was
she would let me have a go
if I wanted

What I really wanted was to go over to her
and give the swing a push
with my hands
so that she
could climb a little higher
in the air

but after thinking it over
I thought better of it

[2002]

91

Longing or Questioning

When I travelled overseas
the first thing to start missing the motherland
was my belly
It began with the first slice of bread
smeared thickly with butter
How come none of the guys
who had been here before me
mentioned
such an obvious thing
so simple an experience?

[2002]

Re: The Nobel Prize – This Is What I Saw

Tomas Tranströmer
sat in the family orchard

Apples hung heavily on the trees
Any one of them

that happened to fall
could have knocked him on the head

All his apples, however
showed great self-discipline

They insisted on not falling
and so resisted ripening

As a result, the owner of the orchard
never got to eat his own fruit

[2002]

One Place I'll Never Visit

Spring there
is nothing like
what we have here
Heaven and earth have swapped places
Winds and waters go opposite ways
There, a kite
flies its owner

[2002]

The Wind Did It!

I saw a strong gust of wind
a gust of wind
blow in from who knows where
It blew
a white plastic table up into the air
The table overturned
and was swept
into a fishing pool
This happened when I was on holiday
two weeks ago
at a holiday village north of the city
There was no witness
apart from me
who saw what actually happened
The people I was staying with
were having an intense discussion
about the death of some male pop star
They didn't notice
that the man who had been sitting at the table
now sinking underwater
was gripped by panic and the knowledge of his innocence
as security guards
grilled him

[2002]

Still

So calm all round
How calm would it need to get
before it drove a man crazy?

At such times
the clocks no longer crack their teeth on time's melon seeds
They choke and refuse to eat

A deaf man
finally hears
a string snap

The stethoscope has also lost its hearing
but can hear that its owner's heart
stopped a long time ago

[2002]

Hearing a Kid Talk about Love on a Moonlit Night during the Mid-autumn Festival

The scene changes from moment to moment
but what shifts is not the moon
whose radiance is even more conspicuous
than its roundness
but the surrounding clouds
in that vast, starlit sky
A ten-year-old boy
lifts his head and watches the bright moon
as the poet once wrote
He says: Love!
He says that love
is a heart
a thumping heart
He says that love
means to pounce on her
so that you get two big smacks
across the face
I am the father of a friend
of this boy
Sitting in the slanting light of the moon in a mushroom-shaped
        pavilion
I was fuckin' bowled over by what I heard

[2002]

Old Tolstoy Ticked Me Off

I watch a live telecast of the Iraq War on CCTV Channel One
with the same enjoyment I had
when I watched last year's World Cup final
worried only that nothing much would happen

There was a movie on Channel 6
During an intermittent ad break in the war telecast
I saw that it was the Hollywood version of Tolstoy's *Anna Karenina*
An aged aristocratic woman said at the top of her voice
'If I lived in Spain
I would go to the bullfights every day!'

I didn't feel so good after that
I wasn't in much of a mood for war then
Old Tolstoy had ticked me off from beyond the grave
and had made his contempt for me clear

[2003]

Gunslinger

When I was young
people noticed
my speedy action

These days
my speed is all they register
The action
happens too quickly

One day
when I'm old
they'll only see the action
but not the speed

In the end
they won't see either: no action
and no speed

[2003]

Beauty • Ugliness

With her dazzling looks, the beautiful actor
bursts into tears as she accepts her Oscar
at the Academy Awards – Clutching her statuette she says:
This is a time for happiness
but it is also a time for sorrow
She adds that she wouldn't be here tonight
if she didn't believe
that art was greater than war

I was
in a restaurant in a small town
somewhere in the east of Northwest of China
watching this scene
on TV
At the same time
a bunch of ugly blokes at a neighbouring table
who were eating instant-boiled mutton
chatted excitedly
in admiration of the American bombardment

[2003]

NOTE: The Chinese word *mei* means 'beauty'; it is also used in the Chinese word for America, *meiguo*.

Face Masks

Once upon a time
whenever I saw someone wearing a face mask
I'd want to know
whether the face beneath it
was good-looking
or plain.
These days
as viruses spread across the globe
whenever I see a face mask
all I want to know
is whether the face beneath it
is crying
or smiling

[2003]

News of SARS

A plague has come
The virus prevails everywhere
The really worrying thing is that
people die every day
Yesterday our national TV
telecast a piece of news
which claimed that
because of timely prevention
and the adoption of appropriate measures
the animals
in the zoo
were all safe
and had not been infected
They lived well
I kept my cool
Not that I didn't hear the news
but I was able
to do the sums:
the little lives of these animals
were worth more
than those of people

[2003]

My Chef, My Master, My Great Peking Grandpa

The most profound lesson I've ever had
about life and writing
I learned
from the old Head Chef at the Egyptian Embassy
He told me how once, as a young man
he had overcooked and burnt a leg of lamb
On the spot, he decided
to make the best of it
and to exploit his mistake
as a brand-new dish
which he called 'Burnt Leg of Lamb'
As it happened, the diners "flipped their lids" over it
Oh, Master!
His Arabic is bloody good
while I can't write a single letter of it
He also mentioned
that bean curd mashed with shallots
made by his wife
and eaten with a glass of *Erguotou*
was the best meal he'd ever tasted
even after a lifetime of cooking
Oh, my Great Peking Grandpa
In his 65° proof voice he said:
'I've served every son of a bitch there is
while she's spent her life serving me.'

[2003]

NOTE: *Erguotou* is a strong spirit made from sorghum.

103

Mikhail Gorbachev

I was thinking of someone
I don't know what he's been up to
these past few years
or how he's been going

I was thinking of someone
who in 1989 visited
what was to me
the last of Beijing

I was thinking of someone
who made me feel so embarrassed
about my leaders when they met with him
He made the mighty look less mighty

I was thinking of someone
and as I thought of him
he happened to appear
on my TV

I was thinking of someone
In the past years he's been travelling the world
and though his wife is dead
he still loves her dearly

I was thinking of someone
He has a red-star birthmark on his bald head
and though the Chinese regard it as an unlucky omen
he actually cares what this block-headed nation thinks

[2003]

Thank You, Father

There was a vast starry sky just like this
in the time of Mao Zedong
and under this sky
there were still people gazing up at it
That summer evening
when my father stayed with me
he told me about
the existence of the cosmos
and about a spaceman
called Gagarin
I was so astonished
my mouth hung open
Thank you, father
You were my god
who made me the cleverest
among the billions
of undernourished and ignorant children
in a corner of the dark kingdom
of North Korea, with a territory of 9.6 million square
kilometres
There I could see no future
but I did see the cosmos

[2003]

NOTE: Yury Alekseyevich Gagarin (1934–68) was a Soviet astronaut.
On 12 April 1961 he became the first human being to travel in space
as well as the first to orbit the Earth.

Dreams

Tonight
you dreamed so many dreams
so many dreams
but in the morning
you could only recall
the contents of one
So you thought: maybe
dreams are cannibalistic –
they devour their own kind

[2003]

Don't Blaspheme Against the Dark

A man lies and describes himself as handsome
A woman, after getting rid of a risk, toys with it
Such illustrious examples are commonplace
in this literate age of ours
but please don't call it a 'dark' age
Darkness – please don't blaspheme against this word
One night when I first started writing
and when I found out my name
had been put onto a certain blacklist
I considered making arrangements to leave the country
and contemplated the possibility
of writing my poetry in prison
I'd locked away my notebooks
in a wooden box
I was ready to take with me at any moment
As I burned my letters from friends
my mood was darkened by the smoke
Back then I still could have passed
for a young man
with a naïve-looking face
Many years have passed since then
The greatest happiness I have ever known in my life
is a simple freedom:
that of no one stopping you from writing

[2004]

Remembering Valentine's Day

In an outdoor teahouse in a plaza
next to an enormous supermarket
I ordered a Coke
and opened my newspaper
oblivious of the fact
it was Valentine's Day

I was reminded by two young women sitting nearby
loaded up with shopping
As they munched away on their BBQ squid
they began chatting about roses
and various men they knew
They were longing for something

Even if the husband of one of the women
rang her on her mobile
he could not have enticed her home
They waited
discussing ways to actively attract
the attentions of several men they knew

I went over to them
with a bunch of roses
and as I stood before them
I looked back to the place
where I had been sitting
and discovered another me there
sipping his drink

[2004]

Dreaming of My Mother the Day
after Mother's Day

She's come back
without the look of sickliness she had when she left us
but one of youthful beauty
One day at dusk
draped in the multi-coloured glow of sunset
she came back from being away
walking with relaxed steps
into our house
in a residential family compound for staff
where we used to live
There stood a double row of one-storey houses
two of which were our home
She's come back
Why did she have to come back
just then?
It was probably for the following reason:
she was off at some hotel attending a conference
and by rights she should have stayed there
but she couldn't help worrying
about my sister and me on our own at home
(my father – he was always away with work)
so she came back
delighting us with the thrill of surprise
This dream
made me break into a cold sweat
and filled me with sadness
Someone has clearly been telling lies
about souls going off to heaven
I'm fully aware that such lies come from
our terrible fear of dying
and from our fear of confronting
cruel reality
The heaven we have invented for ourselves
is, to all intents and purposes, beautiful

beautiful beyond our wildest dreams
yet it is to this world
that all those who die
long to return

[2004]

This Vast Pink Land

Twice this month
friends of mine
have rung me late at night
waking me with a start
a hint of mystery in their voices
and nervousness
just like those underground operatives
back in the days of revolution

Now I can swear
to our old Chairman Mao
at rest in his Memorial Hall
that these two friends of mine
are not underground activists
They're just a couple of young poets
leading normal lives
doing their best
to write good poetry
to employ their mother tongue gracefully

Oh, China
Please allow me to let off a little steam here:
With the passing of so many years
this great land of ours
has changed colour from red to pink
How come you still don't feel
enough of a sense of security
and still go on
rounding up pigeons as if they were dinosaurs?
Aren't you in need
of beautiful white doves and angels
to adorn your azure skies?

[2004]

Urban Landscape

With a cigar in his mouth
and the look of a cheerful talker
Che Guevera turns up in the city centre
on an enormous billboard
Our business leaders have learnt a thing or two
They've started to tire of piddly gimmicks
like 'I love being a woman'
They know that using the images of idealism
to pick the pockets of idealists
is a more sophisticated more fashionable more high-class trick
I happened to pass beneath the billboard with my son
He asked me: *Is that the Big Boss?*
I thought for a moment
then said:
Yes, that's him,
but he's got no money

[2004]

Sun Drunk

Autumn in Chang'an
How rare this afternoon sunlight
Sitting on steps outside a classroom block
at the college where I work
I look like a wine-lover
drunk on sunshine
Half an hour of it has the same effect
as a few shots of alcohol
To my blurred vision
the sunshine
looks like a liquid
coursing through the veins
of a pallid human body
exposed to X-rays

[2004]

Fire

A few
petit bourgeois desires
linger in everyone's minds
I used to think that the most beautiful fire in the world
burned in the fireplace of an old European-style house
but though I've never owned a fireplace like that
I saw the world's most beautiful fire
yesterday in a crematorium south-east of the city
just at that moment when one of my grandfathers
who had lived to the ripe old age of 87
was pushed into the furnace

[2004]

Epiphany

I have no idea when it began
but now every time I watch a cops-and-robbers movie
my sympathies
are always with the crook
After seeing scores of such films
I was suddenly enlightened
and came to see that the tragedy of all criminals
lies in the fact that they fail to detect
the presence of the State
behind every officer of the law they confront
Since then
I no longer care
to regard any one
as my adversary
if the State
stands behind them

[2005]

1972: Lantern Festival

A boy
a boy the same age as me
runs through the night
carrying a red lantern

The next time
I catch sight of him
his lantern
is a ball of flame

It had caught fire
He wailed in despair
as he went on running

In my dreams that night
I saw him again for the third time –

He had turned into a child of fire
in the boundless realm of the night
and in his hand he held
a bright, icy moon
as he ran

[2005]

Spring Snowfall

When I'd got myself ready
to step out into spring
it snowed once more

Each fall of snow
puts me in a good mood
and makes me pray:

Dear God in Heaven
for the suicides who are planning
to jump tomorrow morning
please send another fall of snow just for them –
they'll need it

[2005]

China's Tomb Sweeping Day

Maybe because we're not in the habit
of standing before God
we cannot stand
before the grave of departed loved ones
heads hung in silence
muttering prayers

That's how we are, we Chinese
We're not stuck up –
we're relaxed
On Tomb Sweeping Day
the weather having fined after rain
I sat with the rest of my family
around the grave of my ancestors
built in the shape of a courtyard
It was like sitting down to a special dinner at home
We talked about this and that quite naturally
as if the dead were still with us
and could hear what we said
and answer us with their silences
The fruit we offered them
was, in the end, eaten by the children
They say this brings good luck

For the Chinese
Tomb Sweeping Day is a holiday
a chance to get out of the city and enjoy the spring scenery
together with the ghosts and spirits of the dead
who inhabit these hills and fields

[2005]

118

Bombs and Poetry

Before I left the house
I told my son
that evening
I was going
to the Second Artillery Force College of Engineering
to talk to a group of students learning how to make missiles
about poetry
I told him: what you have to do
is behave yourself
and stay put
until your mother gets home

That evening
after I'd gone
my son must have been confused
He couldn't figure out
how his father
who could only talk about poetry
had the right
to go and lecture
people who would one day be making missiles
Missiles were so awesome
while poetry was stuff like
'Before my bed there is bright moonlight...'

Three hours later
when I got back
my wife was already home
My son was still not in bed
He asked me
if I had seen any missiles
No, I said, and added:
I had seen the money and that was fine
I handed him
an envelope given to me by a colonel

he counted the money in it
then said to me:
Next time, go and give a talk
to people making atom bombs
They're sure to give you even more

[2005]

NOTE: Yi Sha makes a reference here to a classical Tang-dynasty poem,
Li Bai's 'Quiet Night Thoughts' (*Jing ye si*). As Arthur Cooper notes in his
Li Po and Tu Fu, 'This must be the best known now of all Chinese poems...'
The quatrain goes on: 'So that is seems like frost on the ground: / Lifting
my head, I watch the bright moon, / Lowering my head, I dream that I'm
home.' Yi Sha also refers to this poem in 'Hearing a Kid Talk about Love
on a Moonlit Night during the Mid-autumn Festival'.

Bonsai

I've always hated potted plants

They are botanical dwarfs
humans have produced
by imposing on them
the torture of foot-binding
They are
pots and pots
of blood

Things are a little different today
I think of these disgusting bonsai
as I read poems
written by lyric zombies

[2005]

Blind Lane

I learned of the existence of this lane for the blind
only a few years ago – In these few years
I've never seen a blind person
walk on it
(Do they wear sunglasses?)
Neither have I seen any sighted person
dare to set foot on it
Outside the blind lane
there are people everywhere
bustling and hustling
with barely enough room to move
To give space to this yellow blind-lane
seems useless
a vacuum tunnel
but it is the artery
of every main road

[2005]

The Common People

Outside a bank
three people
queue up to use an ATM:
a young female office worker, a casual labourer from the country,
    and myself
I stand between the two of them
that is to say, with the common people
one of them
This then is my position
my standpoint and my outlook
I can only set out from here
Look, I'm not trying to give myself airs
This is a fact
Having read too much of the rubbish written by gurus
I can get a little up myself
and need to be reminded of my place

[2005]

Police Car, Poet, Snow

One wintry day
in a swirl of mud and snow
a police car came screaming
along the street
insufferably arrogant
as usual
pushing and shoving
its way through traffic
The funny thing was that
no matter how smug it acted
it could not shake off
the coat of snow that covered it
and made it look identical
to every other car
all crawling like hearses
and that's why it was upset
As it passed by
a poet who happened to be
trudging across the road
got splattered from head to toe
with mud thrown up by its filthy wheels
What he saw
made him suddenly felt like crying
associating what he had just witnessed
with the ambiguous connection
between this police car
belonging to the state
and the idea that
poetry is like snow

[2006]

The Scene Before Me

One evening during the Spring Festival
after some friends and I had eaten and drunk
to our heart's content at a hot-pot restaurant
we moved on to a café
Along the way
smack in the middle of a slow traffic lane
we came across a legless beggar sitting on the ground
talking to someone on his mobile phone
He shouted as if there were no one else around
You could hear that he was wishing someone a Happy New Year
'I'm sure he's making a long-distance call
to a beggar in another province'
'Maybe it's an international call
to a beggar overseas'
I'm sorry! I apologise for the way
my friends and I shot our mouths off like that
It's not that we're heartless or numb in our feelings
No, we're not prejudiced, contemptuous or
trying to offend
It was a way to hide our shock
Really, we just didn't have time
when confronted with a scene of this type
to equip ourselves with the appropriate feelings

[2006]

Spring Day

The window frames
a scene outside
like a painting done in oils
on my wall

In this painting
a retired driver
in radiant spring sunshine
helps his wife learn to walk again
after a serious illness

Me, I sit at my computer
writing what I think will be
a masterpiece
I've already heard
this old driver's story

He's a really capable bloke
who has kept a large family going
just him and his truck
Now he is old
yet he still serves as a walking stick to his wife

Actually, I can see quite clearly
that men like me
want to write our masterpieces
and to play our empty games
because we were born inferior
to real men like him

[2006]

Dinner-table Lies

During the Spring Festival
at a get-together with good friends
something I said in my drunkenness
was taken as gospel truth:
I said: 'Before I turned 30
I survived the ordeal of beauty's enchantment
Before I turned 40
I'd made it past the lure of fame and fortune
Now, damn it, I was trying to get beyond my fear of life and
        death
Yours truly wasn't afraid of life
so what was there to fear from dying?
My friends took this
as gospel truth
and they respected me for what I said
Truth is, I was telling lies
Truth is, I've never got beyond any of these things

[2006]

I'm a Law-abiding Citizen: I'm Not Afraid of Anyone!

Every time I go out for a walk
and see an armoured van
parked outside the bank
I stop suddenly
and make an abrupt detour

Once or twice however
I've noticed it too late
to turn back
so I force myself
to keep walking
and this makes me seem like a thief
even without stealing

Although I get close enough
to catch a glimpse
of the face of the security guard
dimly visible
within his helmet
and see the wisps of beard on his chin
as well as the dark, menacing gun
that looks like a hard, straining snake
deep down I feel assured
because I know perfectly well

that I look nothing like
any of those infamous bank robbers
Before I did, I'd have to shave off all my pubic hair
and stick it all over my face

[2006]

Practising to Become a Recluse

The flowers in the courtyard have blossomed

My first thought
when I noticed this
was –

they're flowering on the hillsides

I kid you not:
I'm so practised I've already become a recluse

[2006]

Spring's Breast Cancer Disaster

Before they took you into the operating theatre
you lay there on the trolley
and said to your closest girlfriend
'If I wake up to find
my two treasures are gone
that'll mean I've got cancer'
As you spoke you made a gesture with both hands
across your chest

You never breathed a word of this
to me – your husband
You were aware that if anything needed signing
I'd be the one to sign it
Do you trust me with every decision
I have to make?
including the decision
to cut off your beautiful breasts?

I suddenly felt
I would never make it through the spring
I feared the worst
I feared the Old Man in the Sky would turn against me
Already countless times in my mind
I had bowed down before Him
and asked Him to take every thing I had
just as long as He spared my wife's breasts

I stood outside the operating theatre
awaiting sentence
seconds passed like years
An illiterate peasant
grabbed me
and asked me to sign a form for him
but I refused in no uncertain terms

My big peasant brother
suddenly remembered
that he knew how to write his own name
and so the problem was solved
and his wife became
a woman without breasts

Actually, darling
before you went in for your pre-op examination
yesterday afternoon
I happened to see
two women who'd had their breasts removed
through the door of the clinic
left open by mistake
A doctor was changing their bandages
To me, they still looked beautiful
because I had already prepared myself for the worst

[2006]

Spring's Next of Kin

Every spring where the flowers grow
I'm the one asking:
What's that one called?
And that one?
And that?

Afterwards
I forget all the names
A year later
I'm at it again
I ask
and forget all over again
I've been doing this for God knows how long

Yet, compared to the botanists
who know the name of every plant
I have a hunch it's me
who's really
spring's next of kin

[2006]

Born in the Time of Mao

I had no choice
in the shape of my belly-button
and no say
in how unsightly it's turned out

but I have no wish
to be always scraping muck
from it
to show to other people

[2006]

133

Utopia Swelters

With the scorching sun directly overhead
I went out power walking in the street
firstly to try and lose some more weight
and secondly to get a tan
On this day of 40-degree heat
in the grogginess that comes before heat-stroke
I kept on going
and walked into a small village
as if I had walked into a mirage
situated where the city meets the country
a kind of "village in the city"
Wow! Almost the whole village
had turned out
men and women, young and old
lined the streets
Males stripped to the waist
played mahjong at tables they'd set up
They all looked so carefree
as if they were living in Utopia
As a poet
I was about to sing its praises aloud
to say how great everyday life is
and how rich in dignity the traditional life of Chinese people
in its refusal of modernisation
yet I was fully aware that to say so was to kid myself
It was not hard to figure out what really lay behind this
Utopia:
in a village like this
half the houses could not afford air-conditioning
and the half that did
just wanted to save on power

[2006]

Melons in Plague Proportions

Ever since my wife said
that water melons were everywhere this summer
and since one of the melon farmers who went bankrupt
committed suicide
we have been going through a large water melon
a day
In all that time
I've hardly touched a drop of H_2O
My son now smells of melon
As the summer passed
the slab of concrete at my place
began to sprout
and is now a melon patch
all because of
the water melon seeds
my son has carelessly spat out everywhere

[2006]

Faith

In a crowd
of men cursing money as a son of a bitch
but sounding as if they were calling to their grandpas
I could see at a glance he was different

His build
was that of a young man
There was sobriety in his face
Surrounded by all this tedious uproar
he knew how to deal with it quietly
and to come to me for conversation

And so on this particular evening
in a crowd of bellies
belonging to food-and-wine friends
so big they looked like women
carrying 7-month-old babies
we swapped ideas
about how to lead a healthy life

Later, we got onto the subject of faith
He told me he was a Catholic
I said: 'I cannot tell
the difference between Catholics and Christians –
I tend to think all faiths
amount to the same thing

'Then tell me, brother, what's your religion?'
'Me? Poetry!'
I was not wrong in my estimation of him
With a knowing laugh he replied:
'Really? That's one of the essential faiths!'

[2006]

Questions for Myself

A panda
appeared on my TV
I lay on the couch
watching it for a long time
I was asking myself:
was the point of my lifetime struggle
just to turn into a fellow like this
and to be treated as a National Treasure
into the bargain?

To grow as fat as a panda
to the point of charming naïvety
To grow as vegetarian as a panda
to the point of nibbling on bamboo
To grow as docile as a panda
to the point of being loved by anyone who saw it
To grow as chaste as a panda
to the point of only mating twice a year

Need I say: my answer was NO (in English!)
I laughed a queer laugh
and immediately changed channels

[2007]

The Red and the White

I think it was
in *Uncle Tom's Cabin*
or some other film about negro slaves
When a black man
says to a white man
'My blood is red, too!'
I felt a sense of recognition
when I heard this
as a young man
and I followed it up
with a brilliant riposte
which I uttered only to myself

Now – at this moment
the reason why
I can say it out loud
is because I have liberated
the poetry of the Yellow Races
from a diabolical slavery
I say to you
in the form of a liberated poem:
The riposte I came up with as a young man was
'And my semen is white, too!'

[2007]

Looking at Van Gogh

This was a pilgrimage
and evidence of the youth
I once had
Drenched with rain
and looking like a drowned rat
I looked at Van Gogh's paintings
Even after a two full hours
I couldn't tear myself away
but what my feelings were
and what massive waves
and storms
battered my heart
I am powerless to describe
and unwilling
to share with anyone

[2007]

It's the Heart, Still the Heart

If you haven't been to Holland you have no way of knowing
how true to life Van Gogh's paintings are
It's not a matter of them resembling reality
There's something in them ordinary people can't see
because when ordinary people look at something
they don't look with their hearts
They are even less able to see the heart of another human being

The Holland Van Gogh painted has a pulse to it
I could see the frames throbbing

[2007]

Backs to the Church

In Rotterdam
it's a common thing to see
doves and pigeons eating together
There's nothing at all surreal about this

In Rotterdam
it's mainly the tramps
who give the birds
something to eat –
this is a discovery I made myself

With their backs to the church
they sit on benches edging the square
handing out bread and chips
to those white angels

As I walked by
I really felt like feeding them too
but I didn't want to make any trouble
and I was afraid that a bird
would nip off my finger, me being a stranger
from foreign parts

And so the following scene took place:
with a shifty look my eyes in my face in my whole expression
I tossed a coin
into a tramp's money tin
It landed with a clink

[2007]

I Dedicate This Poem to Today's World

China's beautiful scenery
Gorgeous women like clouds
My eyes have got it so easy!
But who was the most beautiful woman I saw
on this trip of mine to Europe?
One day
after I'd bought a ticket
at the ticket office
of Rotterdam Central Station
I turned with my ticket in hand
and nearly fainted with shock
The glimpse of the face
of a Muslim woman
obscured by a black burkha
was sufficient to kill

[2007]